Sumiesque

Namiko Yamada

Sumiesque讃

　Sumiesque（スミエスク）は墨の色をしています。墨の歴史は古く、平安貴族は水面に墨を落とし変容する模様を紙に写し取り、墨流しの雅な遊びを楽しみました。

　墨には焦・濃・重・淡・清で表される諸調があり、雪舟とともに、墨の濃淡とぼかしで霧がたちこめた空間に屹立（きつりつ）する松林をかいた長谷川等伯の『松林図』は水墨画の最高傑作です。

墨は「わび、さび」の枯淡や古雅の趣をつたえ、水墨画のみならず茶道や禅、俳諧の理念とも深く結びつき日本の文化、芸術に大きな影響を与えてきました。

　Sumiesqueは美しくてきれいな生の花を模したものではなく、静寂と幽玄を内包したかたちで見る者の心に何かを訴え、思考することを求めています。見る者と対峙し相対的な立場で自己を強く主張します。

　当然ながら枯れない花、アーティフィシャルフラワーであるSumiesqueには生の花と違う特徴があり、クリエーターの感性で創造力を発揮することができます。Sumiesqueは、また、寡黙に見えて実は多彩。墨に五彩ありといわれるようにそこには、雄弁なメッセージがこめられています。

　日本の深い歴史と文化を礎（いしずえ）としてたつSumiesque。その凛とした個性がもつ表現の可能性は無限に広く大きいのです。

ヨシタ　ミチコ

ヨシタ　ミチコ　Michiko Yoshita
1988年㈱カラースペース・ワム設立。商品、建造物、フラワービジネスの色彩提案を行ない、色彩のプロを育成するカラリストスクール・ワムICI代表として、後進の指導にあたっている。主な著書に『ヨシタミチコの色彩術』『色彩のプロを目指すあなたに　色の仕事のすべて』『パーソナルカラー配色ブック』『花色カラーセラピー』（以上誠文堂新光社）など多数。フラワーデコレーター協会理事長。

Sumiesque Praise

Sumiesque uses Chinese ink; it has a long history in Japan. Nobles in Japan's Heian period copied changing figures by brushing Chinese ink onto wet paper to create an elegant marbling effect.

Chinese ink has a harmony which can appear to be burning, dark, heavy, light, and clean. The "Shorinzu" (Pine Forest Screens) is one of the best Chinese ink paintings by Tohaku Hasegawa in the style of Sesshu, within which Chinese ink is used to create shade and gradation in the image of a standing (Kitsuritsu) pine forest in fog.

Chinese ink traditions have a refined simplicity and embody the classical "Wabi" (austere refinement) and "Sabi" (deep mysterious beauty), and significantly influenced Japanese culture and arts beyond the Chinese-ink painting styles, as these traditions also deeply connect with the Japanese tea ceremony, Zen ideals, and poetic concepts.

The Sumiesque style was not to imitate beautiful flowers, through the images of silence and quiet beauty, but to inspire reflection by viewers as these scenes were in opposition to the viewer's own self-assertion.

Naturally, Sumiesque, as artificial flowers, has different characteristics than fresh flowers, and creators are able to exercise their imagination with sensibility. Sumiesque can be multicolored, but colors are generally used with reticence. As there are only five Chinese ink colors, the use is intended to portray eloquence and delicacy.

Sumiesque is the foundation (Ishizue) of Japan's deep-history and culture. The potential of dignity is infinite.

Michiko Yoshita

序 文

　造花の世界において異色の商品グループであり、極めて奥深い静かな色彩空間を演出する「Sumiesque（スミエスク）」。アーティフィシャルフラワーと総称されるさまざまなタイプの造花があるなかで、ポリエステル繊維生地から生まれた花の異端児といえるかもしれません。

　私たちは日本文化を象徴する色彩を持つ墨の世界を受け止め、背負っていると考え、スミエスクと名づけた花たちがさらにその深層を求め続けていくものと思っています。スミエスクを愛してくださる方々にその可能性を想像していただきたく、作品集にまとめました。限られたアイテムからの構成になったため、日本独特の薄墨桜のような色の作品が含まれていないことは心残りではありますが、今後の発展があることを期待いたします。

　スミエスクが開発され日本市場に展開するまでには、多くの方々からご支援を賜りました。CAFFCO社（米国）のJimmy Thompson氏、Lamar Thompson氏のご家族、New Island社（香港）の史 東山氏ご一家は、日本の輸入業者として踏み出した私どもふたりを支え、力と希望を与えていただきました。

　スミエスク生産業者のUCPP社（香港）のPatrick Koo氏、企画制作のさいに墨色の調合見本に多くの時間を費やされたTassie Design社（タイ）のTassenee Nipatkusol氏、Lotus Nipatkusol氏をはじめ、ポリエステル造花の誕生に貢献なされた新房武久氏、空間デザイナーの故岸 宏氏、販売業者の株式会社アスカ商会の企画・営業をはじめ全スタッフたちなど、多くの諸氏に深く敬意と感謝を申し上げます。

山田 裕康

Prologue

"Sumiesque" can be categorized into different artificial flower product groups and is identified by the extremely deep and quietly colored spaces. While there are various types of artificial flowers, "Sumiesque" flowers can be seen as nonconformist as they are created with a polyester-fiber fabric.

Chinese ink colors represent Japanese culture and we believe that the Sumiesque flowers will continue to demonstrate depth and beauty. We want people to love Sumiesque and to imagine its potential; therefore, we have put a collection together which is typical of this style. Unfortunately, this collection has limited items and, therefore, works that have the light Chinese ink cherry blossom colors so specific to Japan are not included; however we expect that such pieces may be included in the future.

We have had big support from many people to develop the Sumiesque Japanese market. Mr. Jimmy Thompson and Mr. Lamar Thompson, their children and other family members from CAFFCO International (US), and the family members of Mr. Shi Tung Shan from New Island Co. (Hong Kong) heartily supported the two of us when starting an import business in Japan and gave us power and hope.

We would also like to thank Mr. Patrick Koo, a Sumiesque producer from UCPP Co. (Hong Kong), Ms. Tassenee Nipatkusol and Ms. Lotus Nipatkusol from Tassie Design (Thailand) who spent a lot of time mixing Chinese ink color samples for the planning and production, Mr. Takehisa Shinbo, who contributed to the development of the artificial polyester flowers, the deceased, Mr. Hiroshi Kishi, who was a spatial designer, and to the staff at the distributor, ASCA Co., we sincerely express our respect and gratitude for their hard work.

Hiroyasu Yamada

C O N T E N T S

CONTENTS

物語

Story

スミエスク ―時空なるもの―

　「月日は百代の過客にして、行かふ年も又旅人也」と芭蕉は『おくのほそ道』の中で、かぎられた時を旅する私たちに自然と人間、人生とは何かを問いかけました。スミエスク―時空なるもの―は、「不易を知らざれば基立ちがたく、流行を知らざれば風新たならず」と『去来抄』で述べた芭蕉のように、時代を超えて続いてゆく永遠性と、新しく生まれながら時代の変化とともに消えてゆくことのありようを捉え、万物流転の定めを時間と空間、つまり「時空なるもの」で表現しています。

　そのテーマのひとつは自然。流れゆく風や雲、光は手で掴むことはできないが、風の音や刻々とかたちを変える雲、光の明暗に私たちの気持ちは左右され力で制御できないものへの憧れは一層つのります。

　それは信仰と同様に神聖なものを仰ぎみるときにいだく畏敬の念にも似て、万古不易と結びつく思いです。不易と対極にあるかにみえて流行も、時間と空間の関係のように人生の豊かさを語る上では欠かせない不即不離の要素といえます。私たちは実りある日々を願っています。その規範となるのは礼節であり、気持ちを鼓舞する雅な彩り。風流を解して趣を味わう心の余裕。この礼・雅・趣が響きあい共鳴しあう調和こそ、豊かに生きることのテーマでしょう。

　日常の生活空間にスミエスクを置いて生まれるのは豊潤な時間と空間。その四次元と三次元のなかを行き来しながら追い求めるのは流れてゆくものと立ちどまるものについての考察。スミエスクは豊かに生きたいと願う真摯な問いに向き合い、いつも応えてくれる讃歌なのです。

Sumiesque — Space-Time —

Basho explained the meaning of nature, humans, and life to those who traveled in "Oku no Hosomichi" (Narrow road to/from the interior), when he wrote "The months and days are the travelers of eternity. The years that come and go are also voyagers." As Basho wrote, "One doesn't discover new lands without consenting to lose sight of the shore for a very long time." in "Kyoraisyo" (Kyorai's Notes). Sumiesque–Space Time– represents the idea that everything is constantly changing in time and space, or "Space-Time," while eternity continues throughout the ages with newly born figures disappearing with the changes in the ages. One of the themes is nature; flowing winds, clouds, or light cannot be caught, but our feelings are aroused by the sound of the wind, the changing clouds, the brightness and darkness of light, and our longing for something that we cannot control. It is similar to the feeling of awe we have when we look at a holy object and the faith we have that it is linked to an eternal unchanging. Constancy is the opposite of fashion; however, fashion cannot be too faithful, or too free, just as in the relationship between time and space. We wish for a prosperous life. Politeness and elegance can be the norm and are colored to inspire our feelings. A relaxed mind enjoys good taste through the adoption of refinement, and this politeness/elegance/taste fits with the theme of an abundant life. Time and space can be experienced by placing Sumiesque in your everyday living space. The movement back and forth between the three and four-dimensional spaces represents the ebb and flow of life around. Sumiesque is a song of praise, which confronts and responds to the needs of people who want an abundant life.

風を刻む

風は気配

誰も風を見たことがない

つかむこともできない

でもたしかに草木のゆれる音がする

心地のよい風もあれば嵐を呼ぶ風もある

風は移りかわる季節の表情をつたえる

E_ng_ra_vi_ng W_in_d

Wind is a sign.

Nobody sees the wind.

Nobody can catch it.

However, people can certainly hear the sound of the trees and plants.

There is a comfortable wind, as well as a tempestuous wind.

Winds represent the differences in the changing seasons.

疾 風
<ruby>はやて</ruby>

Sudden Wind (Hayate)

凪 の 予 感

Premonition of Calm

激しい貌（かお）もある

Aspect of Intense Appearance（Kao）

花風が

春を運ぶ

Flower Wind delivers Spring

薫風
<small>くんぷう</small>

時間は
ゆっくりと
流れる

Light Breeze（Kunpu）
Time Passes Slowly

風をながめる

Gazing at the Wind

風に手をかざす

Passing Hands over the Wind

風をとめる

Stopping the Wind

葉風は
花を集める

Breeze through the Leaves Collects Flowers

色 な き 風 の 季 節

Season of Wind without Color

神立の風の奥行は深い

Wind within Thunder (Kandachi) Leaves a Deep Impression

Reading the Clouds

A cloud has a shape.

A cloud is constantly changing its shape.

Not only does the shape change, but the color tones move from happy and anxious; from white to gray to black.

Nothing is more attractive than white clouds in a blue sky, as this excites our feelings.

雲をよむ

雲はかたち

変幻自在にかたちをかえる雲

かたちだけではなく、白、灰、黒と

雲の色調に一喜一憂するときもある

青い空に浮かぶ白い雲ほど

あこがれをかきたてるものはない

<ruby>豊旗雲<rt>とよはたぐも</rt></ruby>が
吉兆をつくる

Banner Clouds (Toyohatagumo)
Bring Good Omens

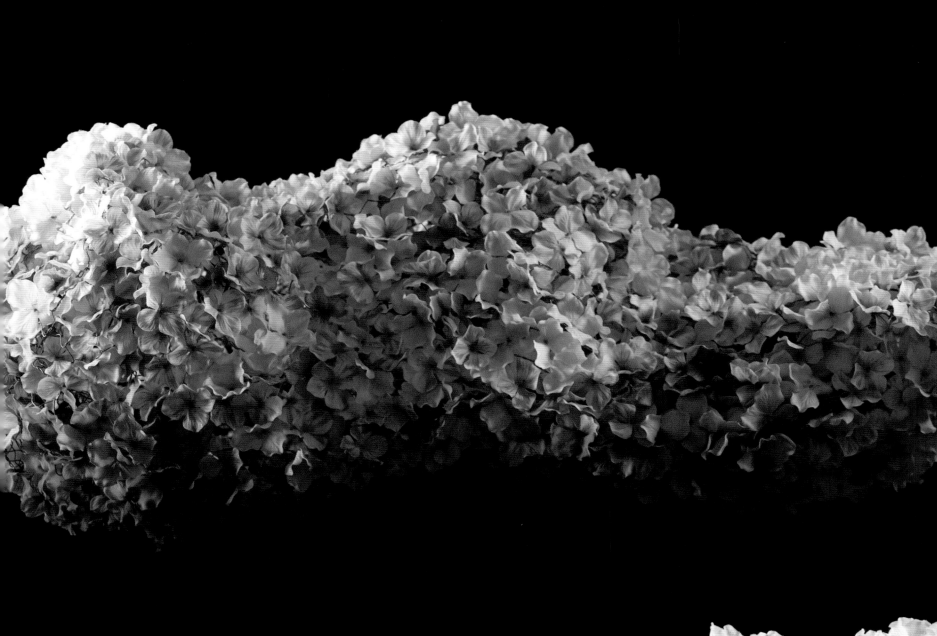

綿雲は
鈍色（にびいろ）を払う

Fleecy Clouds Brush off the Dark Gray（Nibiiro）

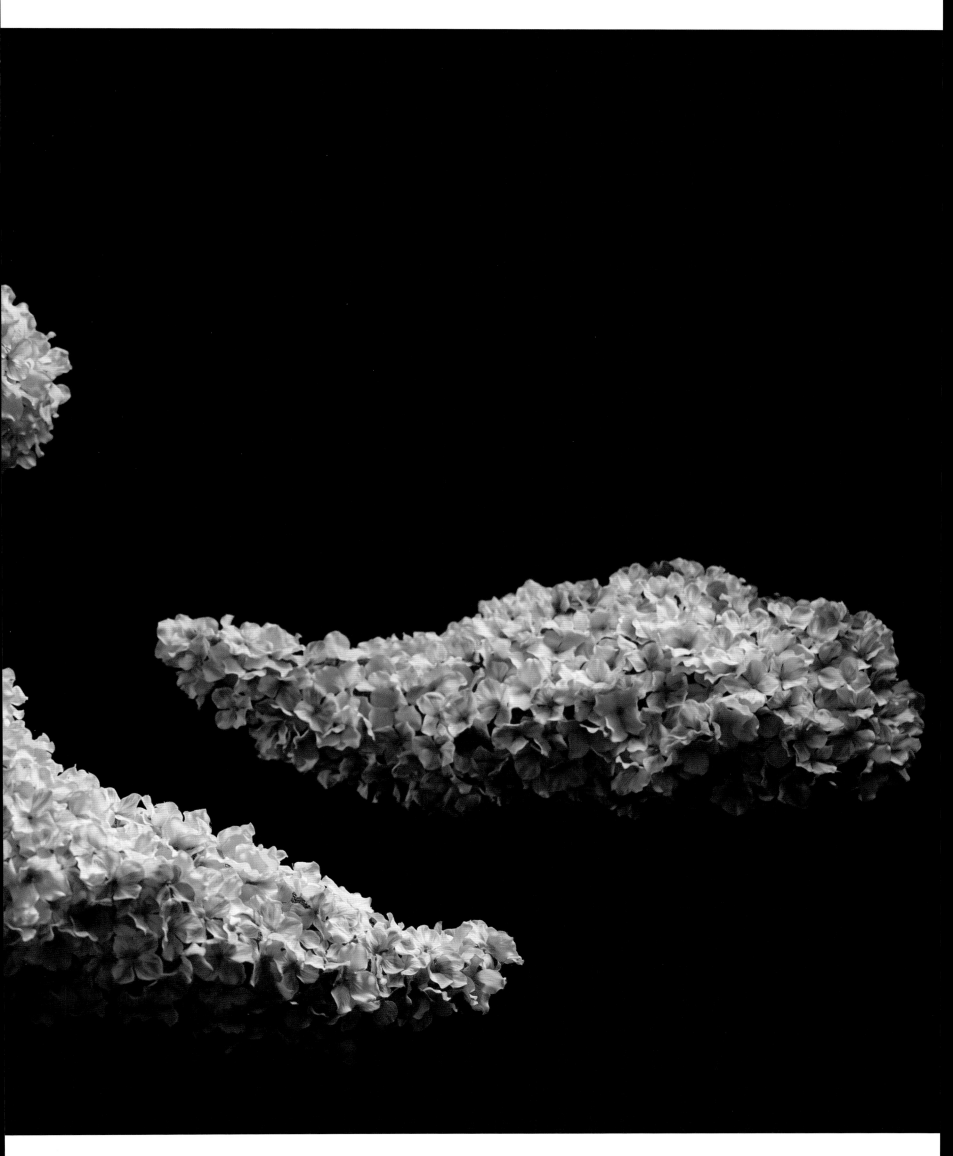

雲 海

雲 に 言 葉 は い ら な い

Sea of Clouds / No Word is Required for Clouds

羊雲に青が揺れる

Blue is Swaying in the Floccus Clouds

積 乱 雲　　影 が 動 く

Cumulonimbus Clouds / The Shadows are Moving

蝶々雲

陽を受けて
雲は
饒舌になる

Butterfly Clouds
Drink the Sunlight and Become Garrulous

朧雲

（おぼろぐも）

月を宿す雲もある

Altostratus Clouds (Oborogumo) / Some Clouds Harbor the Moon

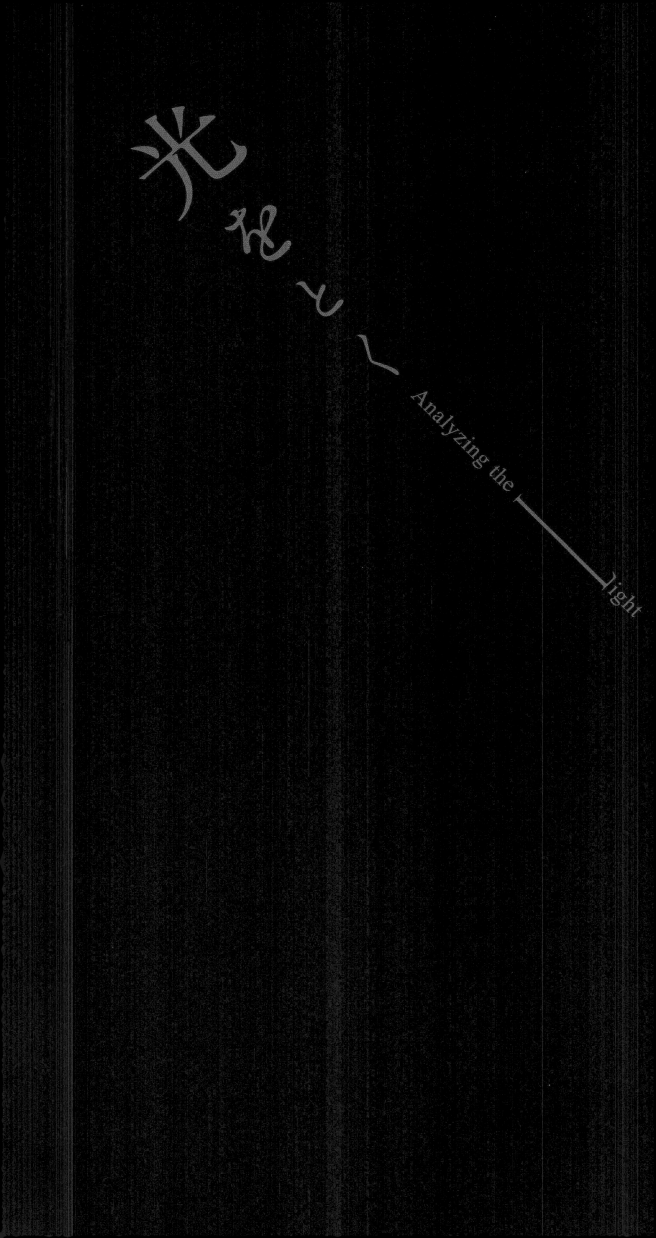

光はロマネスク

明るい光はガラスの透明さを際立たせ

シルクロードの旅の記憶と重なる

暗い光に溶けたのは静謐な思索の時間

ボードレールの憂鬱は冷たいガラスの先にあり

夜の光は無意識の意識と響鳴して感性を刺激する

Light is Romanesque.

Bright light emphasizes the transparency of glass and

is wrapped with the memory of the Silk Road.

What is dissolved into dark light becomes the subject of tranquil speculation.

Baudelaire's depression sits upon the top of the cold glass.

Night-light stimulates subtlety by sympathizing

with the consciousness in the unconsciousness.

黄昏
たそがれ

落ちてゆく時間

Twilight (Tasogare) / Falling Time

はくめい
薄 明

明 る い 静 寂

Faint Light (Hakumei) / Bright Silence

幻日
<ruby>げんじつ</ruby>

光 の 色 を 探 す

Mock Sun (Genjitsu) / Investigating Light and Color

白夜

透明な夜の感触

Night under the Midnight Sun / The Feeling of a Transparent Night

有 明

飛 び 散 る 光

Dawn / Sparking Light

夜会

陽気な夜もある

Evening Party / One Cheerful Evening

空を

The Knowing Ku,vacancy

空は色即是空

この世は仮のもの

かたちあるものはすべて消えてゆく

万物流転　確かなかたちはなにもない

しかし　定めのない空を見据えたとき

かすかに見えてくるものがある

知る

Ku is all vanity.

This world is temporary.

Tangible things are disappearing.

Everything is constantly changing. No certain shapes exist.

However, something can be faintly seen,

when people stare at an uncertain Ku.

Far away Object / Contemplation of Distance

かなたにあるもの
想いを馳せる

Far away Object / Contemplation of Distance

ガルシンと埴輪
踊るそして
つながる

Garshin and the Clay Images Dancing and Connecting

祈りのとき
円空と出会え

Time for Prayer / Meeting Enk

時を結ぶ

仕舞っておきたいこと

Linking Time / A Thing to Store

天空に立つ

心が澄んでゆく

Standing the Airy Region / The Heart Becomes Clear

煩 悩

悟りをめざす

Worldly Passions / Aiming for Spiritual Awakening

Gen, delicate beauty, subtle and profound

玄 の 本 質

The Essence of Gen

<ruby>茫漠{ぼうばく}</ruby>

黙って向き合う

Vagueness (Boubaku) / Confronting in Silence

雅を装う

Wearing Elegant Clothing

雅は気品

金糸銀糸で織りなされた錦模様は

華やぎをつくり気持ちを鼓舞するが

つややかさをおさえて凛とした趣もまた

花の矜持を確かなものにする

Elegance means dignity.

Brocade patterns made by weaving golden and silver yarns creates

brilliance and excites people's feelings; however

dignified taste with a controlled sheen

also ensures the flower's pride.

雅

華やぎをかいま見る

Elegance / A Glimpse of Brilliance

趣

竹 取 の 庭 に 遊 ぶ

Taste / Playing in the Garden of the Bamboo Cutter

礼

凛 と し て 立 つ

Politeness / Dignified Standing

響はハーモニー

昼と夜のあわいもさりながら

夜のしじまと昼の喧騒

夜の闇と白日の光が示すように

静と動、陰と陽が互いに引きたてあい

それぞれがバランスよく存在を主張する

Sound means harmony.

Between daytime and night,

the night silence quarrels with the daytime.

As darkness in the night and broad daylight indicate,

silence/movement and positive/negative emphasize each other and

Individually insist their existence is well balanced.

Creating So

響

を
つくる

金属との融合
共鳴しあうもの

Harmony in Metal
Sympathizing Together

どこまでも
上昇してゆく

Everywhere and Continuing to Rise

どこまでも
上昇してゆく

Everywhere and Continuing to Rise

慕情

忘れえぬ面影

Longing / Unforgettable Images

強靭 なるオブジェ

Strong Objet d'art

強さに平伏すときがある

Sometimes, People Prostrate Themselves before Power

射止める

Obtaining

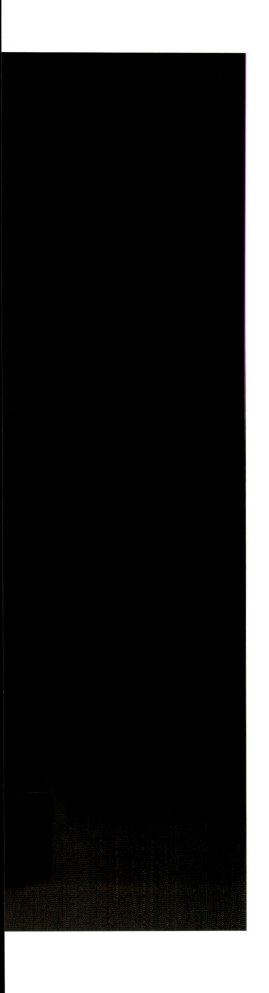

飛 翔

よ だ か の 星

Flight / Nighthawk Star

流れゆく思念

Flowing Thought

影のない時間

Time without Shadow

花を置く

Placing a Flower

花は情操

花は空間をゆるぎない空間にかえ

［時］の印象をのこす

花は喜怒哀楽の情感と結びつき

思い出は今と昔を自由に往ききする

Flowers are sentiment.

Flowers steady a space and leave a "Time" impression.

Flowers are linked in turn to both happiness and anxiety.

Memory goes freely back and forth from the present to the past.

悦 ば し い 光 景
日 々 の か た ち

Delightful Scene / Daily Form

陽だまり

ありふれた一瞬

Sunny Spot / Common Moment

音のないところ
気持ちが降り立つ

Place without Sound / Exciting

青い刻
古い言葉と出会う

Words that I haven't heard for a long time

清冽<ruby>せいれつ</ruby>

微動だにしないときもある

Clear (Seiretsu) / Moment without Movement

白い花　白のかたちは記憶にのこらない

White Flower / White Shape is not Memorable

白いとき　黙っている時間

White Moment / Silent Time

雲が湧き風は流れる
そして光も宿る
かすみたつ山なみを庭にして
今日がはじまる

Clouds Arise, Wind flows and Light Dwells
The day starts anew as I look over a misty mountain range, behind the garden

そえがき
Description

風 を 刻む   Engraving Wind

▍ 疾風   Sudden Wind (Hayate)

▍ 凪の予感   Premonition of Calm

▍ 激しい貌もある   Aspect of Intense Appearance (Kao)

炎に焼かれ深くひび割れた器。それに添うスミエスク。
風が激しく吹き荒れ、やがておとずれる静けさ。
そして、ふたたび激しい雷鳴が響きわたる。

Vessels that burned in flames and were deeply cracked. Sumiesque goes with it.
The wind blows fiercely, and eventually tranquility comes.
But the violent thunder will resonate again.

▍ 花風が春を運ぶ   Flower Wind delivers Spring

花風は桜の盛りのころに吹き、たくさんの花を運ぶ舟が水面に影を映して進む。

The flower wind blows when the cherry blossoms are in full bloom,
and a boat carrying countless flowers moves onward as its shadow is reflected on the surface of water.

▍ 薫風   時間はゆっくりと流れる   Light Breeze (Kunpu) / Time Passes Slowly

初夏の若葉青葉を吹き抜けたのはやわらかく穏やかな風。

A soft and gentle breeze blows through the young green leaves of early summer.

▍ 風をながめる   Gazing at the Wind

▍ 風に手をかざす   Passing Hands over the Wind

▍ 風をとめる   Stopping the Wind

わたしがどこで生まれどのように暮らしてきたかは、どうでもよい。
大切なのは、その地でわたしがなにをしたかである。
ジョージア・オキーフ
オキーフが暮らしたニューメキシコには、今日も砂漠の乾いた風が吹いているのだろうか
風をながめ、風に手をかざし、風に手をとめたオキーフは
直感をとらえ刺激に充ちた風景画や抽象画をかいた。
風を心に刻むこと。
それはジョージア・オキーフへの永遠の讃歌。

ジョージア・オキーフ　1887年―1986年　アメリカを代表する女流画家
　　　　　　　　　　　　　　　　生命の根源に眼差しをむけた孤高の人。
　　　　　　　　　　　　　　　ジョージア・オキーフ美術館
　　　　　　　　　　　　　　　（ニューメキシコ州　サンタフェ）

It doesn't matter where I was born and raised.

What matter is what I accomplished there.

Georgia O'Keeffe

I wonder whether that dry desert wind where O'Keeffe lived in New Mexico still blows even now.

She watched that wind, let it run through her hands, even stopped it with her hands.

With a keen instinct, she drew stimulating landscapes and made abstract paintings.

That wind was engraved into her mind.

That's a hymn dedicated to the eternal memory of Georgia O'Keeffe.

Georgia O'Keeffe (1887-1986)　　Famous American female painter.

She was a rather aloof person who had the ability to look at the roots of life.

Georgia O'Keeffe Museum

(Santa Fe, NM)

❘　葉風は花を集める　　Breeze through the Leaves Collects Flowers

涼しくなる秋のころに吹き抜けていく風。
スミエスクのコスモスは墨、桜、桜鼠、茜、銀鼠の花色でさらに際立つ
季節をつくる。

The breeze is blowing in autumn, making the weather cooler.

Cosmos flowers in Sumiesque have many colors, such as Chinese ink, cherry blossom, light pinkish gray, madder red and light bluish gray, which make the season more distinguished.

❘　色なき風の季節　　Season of Wind without Color

白秋は秋の季節。秋の韻きはコスモスのかすかな色あいのなかにある。
秋はなぜかもの寂しい。芭蕉は　石山の石より白し秋の風　と詠んでいる。

松尾芭蕉　1644年—1694年　俳人。

Hakusyu (white autumn) means the autumn season. The spirit of autumn can be seen in the faint tint of the cosmos.

Autumn is a somewhat melancholic season. Basyo's haiku reads, "Whiter far than all the stones of Ishiyama – the autumn wind".

Matsuo Basyo (1644-1694) Haiku poet

❘　神立の風の奥行は深い　　Wind within Thunder (Kandachi) Leaves a Deep Impression

神立は雷のこと。
雷鳴をともなって吹く風はすべてを拒否する烈しさをもっている。
背景の岩と枯草から荒々しい厳しさを垣間みる。

Kandachi means thunder.

The wind is fierce when it's paired with thunder, scattering everything in its wake.

Its severity can be seen in the rocks and withered grass in the background.

雲をよむ　Reading the Clouds

▌ 豊旗雲が吉兆をつくる　Banner Clouds (Toyohatagumo) Bring Good Omens

旗のようにたなびき壮麗さを讃えた豊旗雲によい兆しを予感する。

わたつみの豊旗雲に入日さし今夜の月夜さやけくありこそ　　　『万葉集』

Spotting a wonderful Toyohatagumo cloud with plumes that flow like banners is a sign of good fortune.

Seeing the sun shining brightly behind the Toyohatagumo cloud tells me that the moon will be out in splendor tonight. (Manyoshu)

Emperor Tenji (626 - 671) Emperor during the Asuka period

▌ 綿雲は鈍色を払う　Fleecy Clouds Brush off the Dark Gray (Nibiiro)

鈍色は『源氏物語』にも登場する喪の色。陽が沈んだ後の闇をあらわす。

白は新生 そしてあこがれ。綿雲の白は鈍色をふり払い希望をいだかせる。

Nibiiro (dark gray) is a color of mourning that is mentioned in the *tale of Genji*. It represents the darkness that comes after sunset.

White represents re-birth and longing. White cottony clouds whisk away the dark gray and inspire wishes.

▌ 雲海　雲に言葉はいらない　Sea of Clouds / No Word is Required for Clouds

すべてを包み込むように広がる雲を前にすると言葉が消えてしまう。

言葉は追いつかない。

There is no word when we gaze upon the magnificence of the clouds as they spread out and envelop everything.

There is no word to represent such feelings.

▌ 羊雲に青が揺れる　Blue is Swaying in the Floccus Clouds

雲は空の青、海の青をうばい漂う。

青は露草色、花色とも呼ぶ。

露草の古名は月草または鶏頭草。

露草の摺り染めは水に遭うとすぐ褪せてしまう。

As the clouds drift by, they seem to steal even the blue from the sky and the seas.

Blue is the color of dayflowers, and it is also called the "flower color".

An old name for dayflowers was Tsuki gusa (moon grass) or Keito gusa (cockscomb grass).

Dayflower-dyed cloth fades as soon as it touches water.

▌ 積乱雲　影が動く　Cumulonimbus Clouds / The Shadows are Moving

冬の稲妻は影が深い。

積乱雲は嵐の予感をはらんでいる。

Winter lightning has deep shadows.

Cumulonimbus clouds herald the storms.

蝶々雲　陽を受けて雲は饒舌になる

Butterfly Clouds Drink the Sunlight and Become Garrulous

蝶が舞うように雲は流れ、影も動く。
そして時を忘れて気ままなおしゃべりは続く。

Clouds flow as butterflies flutter, even their shadows move.
They forget all about time and continue their chattering.

朧雲　月を宿す雲もある

Altostratus Clouds (Oborogumo) / Some Clouds Harbor the Moon

雨の前兆ともいわれる朧雲は、昼間は花ぐもり夜は朧月夜をもたらす。
夜空一面に広がった雲は、あたかも月を宿したかのように見える。

Altostratus clouds are said to be a harbinger of rain. They bring somber weather during the day and a hazy moon at night.
The clouds spread out all over the night sky and look as if they are harboring the moon.

光をとく　Analyzing the Light

黄昏　落ちてゆく時間　Twilight (Tasogare) / Falling Time

夕暮れは耽美的。
アール・ヌーヴォーを代表するガラス工芸家ドーム兄弟の器が
暮れなずむ時を表現している。
ドーム兄弟は19世紀から20世紀初頭にかけてエミール・ガレとともに活躍し
植物などの自然描写で独自の装飾手法を確立した。

ドーム兄弟　オーギュスト・ドーム　1853年—1909年
　　　　　　アントナン・ドーム　1864年—1930年

The Daum brothers actively worked from the 19th century to the early 20th century, which was the same era as that of Emile Galle.
They established a unique decorative technique for depicting natural objects, such as plants.

The Daum brothers / Auguste Daum 1853 - 1909
Antonin Daum 1864 - 1930

薄明　明るい静寂　Faint Light (Hakumei) / Bright Silence

黒の花が覆った夜。
光をうけたガラスの中で、夜はゆっくりと明けてゆく。

Black flowers cover the night.
The night slowly fades to gray in this glass when it receives the energy of light.

幻日　光の色を探す　Mock Sun (Genjitsu) / Investigating Light and Color

過ぎし日のそこはかとなき物思い……とボードレールがつぶやく。
光を求めて闇に溶けない青もある。

ボードレール　1821年—1867年　フランスの詩人
代表作『悪の華』『信天翁』『パリの憂鬱』

The bell reminds me of distant old days... Baudelaire whispers.
Blue meets light, and even the darkness cannot completely overcome it.

Charles Baudelaire (1821 - 1867)　French poet
Masterpieces: *Flowers of Evil, The Albatross, The Melancholy of Paris*

白夜　透明な夜の感触　Night under the Midnight Sun / The Feeling of a Transparent Night

『白夜』はペテルブルクを舞台にしたドストエフスキーの短編小説。
それは、薄明りがつづく真夜中に出会った青年と少女のはかない恋。
時の流れはたゆたう煙のように消えてゆく。

ドストエフスキー　1821年—1881年　ロシアを代表する小説家。
代表作『罪と罰』『白痴』『悪霊』
『未成年』『カラマーゾフの兄弟』

"White Nights" is a short story by Dostoevsky, set in St.Petersburg.
In the story, a young man meets a girl under the embrace of twilight, and they fall into a fleeting romance.
The flux of time diminishes like smoke.

Fyodor Dostoevsky (1821 - 1881)　Famous Novelist from Russia
Masterpieces: *Crime and Punishment, The Idiot, The Devils, A Raw Youth, The Brothers Karamazov.*

有明　飛び散る光　Dawn / Sparking Light

燃えあがり燃えつきた夜の幻想は光の中でとどまっている。

The burned-out remains of a night time fantasy can still be seen in the light.

夜会　陽気な夜もある　Evening Party / One Cheerful Evening

葡萄酒の深い香りと話し声。踊りの輪にドレスがゆれて
きらびやかな夜会はつづく。

The deep aroma of wine and the chattering of voices. Dresses sway back and forth in a frenzy of dancing. The gorgeous soirée goes on.

空を知る The Knowing Ku ,vacancy

▌ かなたにあるもの　想いを馳せる　Far away Object / Contemplation of Distance

眺める場所によって表情が違うモン・サン＝ミッシェルにその時どきの
気持ちを重ねてみる。回廊を巡って感じた中庭の神秘はいつも記憶の中にある。

モン・サン＝ミッシェルはフランス西海岸サン・マロ湾上に浮かぶ小島。
カトリック巡礼の聖地のひとつ。

The expression of Mont-Saint-Michel varies depending on where you view the piece from, and my feelings overlap each time
I will always remember the mysterious feeling that I had in the courtyard while walking around in a corridor

Mont-Saint-Michel is an island in the Saint-Malo Bay on the west coast of France.
It is one of the sacred places for Catholic pilgrimages.

▌ ガルシンと埴輪　踊るそして　つながる　Garshin and the Clay Image / Dancing and Connecting

『赤い花』に代表されるガルシンは19世紀を生きたロシアの作家。
純粋で研ぎ澄まされた感受性ゆえに苦悩するガルシンは、光のなかで無垢な埴輪と救われたように踊っている。

Garshin was a Russian writer famous for the story "The Red Flower", who lived in the 19th century.
Due to his pure and finely honed sensitivity, Garshin was in anguish. He appears to be healed when dancing with a clay image of purity in the light.

▌ 祈りのとき　円空(えんくう)と出会う　Time for Prayer / Meeting Enku

日本各地を巡り、12万体の仏像を彫ったとされる円空。
慈愛に満ちたほほ笑みと荒削りの木彫りの仏像は「円空仏」と呼ばれた。

円空　1632年−1695年

It is believed that Enku traveled throughout various districts of Japan and carved 120,000 Buddha statues.
These roughly carved statues full of smiles and loving expressions are called 'Enku Buddha"

Enku 1632 - 1695

▌ 時を結ぶ　仕舞っておきたいこと　Linking Time / A Thing to Store

遙か昔と今とを一瞬にして結びつけるもの。
墨絵に描かれた600年前の清水寺とスミエスクが結ばれ
一体感を生み出すことに心が動かされた。

What is it that can connect ancient times and the present-day instantaneously?
I was moved when I found out that the ink painting of the Kiyomizu Temple,
which was drawn 600 years ago, and Sumiesque were combined and brought such a sense of harmony.

▌ 天空に立つ　心が澄んでゆく　Standing the Airy Region / The Heart Becomes Clear

果てしない空や海を目の前にしたとき、その偉大さに心は純化されていく。

When one sees the endless sky and sea in front of him, one is purified by their greatness.

▌ 煩悩　悟りをめざす　Worldly Passions / Aiming for Spiritual Awakening

煩悩とは欲望のこと。多くの人々は迷いから抜け出せない悩みを持っている。
悟りは厳しい修行を重ね心の迷いを解き放ち真理と向き合うこと。

Bonno means the desire for worldly things. Most people are full of anxiety and unable to escape from their worldly attachments.
An awakening can be obtained after repetitive strict training, which allows one to be free from such worldly desires and enables one to confront the truth.

▌ 玄　Gen, delicate beauty, subtle and profound

▌ 玄の本質　The Essence of Gen

玄は黒のこと。紀元前6世紀から紀元前3世紀の中国で生まれた五行思想では北の方位を示し季節は冬を表わす。
玄は黒、光を吸収し反射することなくすべてを包括する色の力は、強制や抑圧を跳ね返す強さと挑戦力をもっている。

Gen means blackness. In the five elements theory prevalent in China from the sixth century BC to the third century BC,
Gen indicates north and also represents winter. Gen absorbs light rather than reflecting it, and it encompasses everything.
It contains the spirit of challenge and the power to repel imposition and oppression.

▌ 茫漠（ぼうばく）　黙って向き合う　Vagueness (Boubaku) / Confronting in Silence

自分の前にあるつかみどころのない広がりのなかには、ゆらぎがある。直視したくない現実や闇もある。
遠くに消えなずむ想いもある。

In the elusive extent of space before me, there are fluctuations.
There are also the reality and the darkness which is unbearable to face to.
And there is a thought to fade to far away as well.

雅を装う Wearing Elegant Clothing

▌ 雅　華やぎをかいま見る　Elegance / A Glimpse of Brilliance

平安王朝の美を彩る色と香り。装束は「襲の色目」と呼ばれ、
宮廷に集う女人たちは自然を模した色合わせで装いのセンスを競い合った。
『源氏物語』には「御簾のうち匂いいとも深き黒方にしみて名香の煙もほのかなり」とあり、
香りもまた気高く優雅な美意識に支えられていた。

Colors and fragrances represent the beauty of the Heian period. The costume is also called "layered colors".
Women who took part in the court life of the Heian period competed with each other by matching the colors in their costumes.
attempting to mimic the colors of nature.
In the *Tale of Genji* it is stated,"Incense filled the inside of a bamboo screen, and the subtle smell of smoke from the incense sticks wafted up".
Fragrance was considered to be noble, which also supported the esthetic consciousness of the time.

▌ 趣　竹取の庭に遊ぶ　Taste / Playing in the Garden of the Bamboo Cutter

花鳥風月の趣、とりわけ月の満ち欠けの神秘性と月の光の美しさは、多くの詩歌によまれ物語がうまれた。
なかでも平安初期の『竹取物語』は、月をめぐる日本最古の物語。
満月の夜に月へ帰って行った「かぐや姫」の謎は永遠に月へのあこがれをかきたてる。

The charms of the beauty of nature, including flowers, birds, the wind, and the moon, and especially the wonder of the waxing and waning of the moon,
and the beauty of its light, have been expressed in many poems and stories throughout time.
Among them *The Tale of the Bamboo-Cutter*, written in the Heian period, is the oldest story that contains the theme of the moon.
The mystery of the "Moon Princess", who went back to the moon on the night of a full moon, stirs our eternal longing for the moon.

▌ 礼　凛として立つ　Politeness / Dignified Standing

礼とは古来人が生きてゆくときに欠くことのできない考え方であり仕来り。
その礼に法った節度ある振舞いと凛とした佇まいは、すべての礎となるもの。
気品と礼節は人をひきつけてやまない要素。

Rei means courtesy and was a way of thinking and a practice, which was indispensable for people who lived in ancient times.
Moderate behavior and a dignified appearance that conforms to good manners and etiquettes are the foundation of life.
Grace and courtesy are elements that will always attract people.

響をつくる　Creating Sound

▌ 金属との融合　共鳴しあうもの　Harmony in Metal / Sympathizing Together

▌ どこまでも　上昇してゆく　Everywhere and Continuing to Rise

造花のやわらかさと金属の硬さ。また高さのあるものと低いもの。
ハードな金属がその持ち味を生かせるのは、スミエスクが異素材とも融合することができるため。
対極にあるものは対極にあるからこそ引き立て合い、調和が生まれる。

The softness of artificial flowers and the hardness of metal represent highs and lows.
Because Sumiesque can synthesize any kind of material, the hardness of metal represents this characteristic effectively.
Two things at the opposite end of the spectrum help each other, to increase their attractiveness, creating harmony between them.

▌ 慕情　忘れえぬ面影　Longing / Unforgettable Images

蝶のようにさまざまな想いが胸のなかに降りてくる。
鉄のオブジェは彫刻家の故山本英行氏の作品。
いつも忘れえぬ面影がそこにある。

My mind springs into action, like the spiraling of butterflies.
The iron object was created by a sculptor, the late Hideyuki Yamamoto.
It will always hold unforgettable images.

▌ 強靭なるオブジェ　Strong Objet d'art

▌ 強さに平伏すときがある　Sometimes, People Prostrate Themselves before Power

▌ 射止める　Obtaining

生きてゆく指針を定めたものは強い。
見る向きによって全く異った表情を見せるスミエスク。
素材を分解し組み合わせることで新しいオブジェが生まれる。

One who can find a guide for life is strong.
Sumiesque shows completely different expressions depending on where you view it from.
New objects are born when materials decompose and are combined in a new way.

▌ 飛翔　よだかの星　　　Flight / Nighthawk Star

宮沢賢治の童話『よだかの星』からのイマジネーション。
生きることに絶望したよだかは、命がけで夜空に向かって飛び続け
火の光となって、カシオペヤ座の近くで今も燃え続けている。

宮沢賢治　1896年―1933年　詩人、童話作家。

This is inspired by the fairy tale *The Nighthawk Star*, written by Kenji Miyazawa.
Yodaka (Nighthawk) felt it was hopeless to continue living, so he tried desperately to fly up into the night sky.
He became like the light of the stars, and his flame continues to burn near Cassiopeia

Kenji Miyazawa (1896 - 1933)　Poet, fairy tale writer.

▌ 流れゆく思念　　Flowing Thought

▌ 影のない時間　　Time without Shadow

流れてしまった時間は影を持たない。想いをたぐりよせることしかできない。

Time flows by so quickly, even shadows cannot form under it. Everything is but a passing thought in the flow.

花 を 置 く　Placing a Flower

▌ 悦ばしい光景　日々のかたち　　Delightful Scene / Daily Form

▌ 陽だまり　ありふれた一瞬　　Sunny Spot / Common Moment

▌ 音のないところ　気持ちが降り立つ　　Place without Sound / Exciting

よろこびのかたちはさまざまにある。光が注ぐ窓辺の明るさ。
そして大切な人を偲ぶ空間、そこに流れる静寂。

There are many ways of expressing joy.
The brightness of a sun-soaked window pane or
the peaceful silence of a place where fond memories of friends and families were shared.

青い刻　古い言葉と出会う　Words that I haven't heard for a long time

『青鞜(せいとう)』の創刊時に「元始女性は太陽であった」と辞を寄せた平塚らいてう。
創造的な仕事と向き合う女性のエネルギーは、時代を超えて続いてゆく。

平塚らいてう　1886年―1971年　思想家・評論家・作家。戦前と戦後にわたる女性解放運動家。
雑誌『青鞜』1911年発刊

In the first issue of *Seito*, a comment by Raicho Hiratsuka reads, "The sun was a woman in ancient times".
The energy of women who are involved in creative work has been inherited over the ages.

Raicho Hiratsuka (1886 - 1971) Thinker, critic, writer. She was a women's liberation activist in prewar and postwar Japan.
The magazine *Seito* was first published in 1911.

清冽　微動だにしないときもある
Clear (Seiretsu) / Moment without Movement

沈思黙考するための和のしつらえ。空気は動かない。

Japanese-style atmospheres were created to aid contemplation. The air does not move.

白い花　白のかたちは記憶にのこらない
White Flower / White Shape is not Memorable

白いとき　黙っている時間
White Moment / Silent Time

光をイメージする明るい白は雑念を払う。
喜怒哀楽の感情をおさえて思考を統一する。

The brightness of white with the image of light casts away worldly thoughts.
Refrain from emotions like delight, anger, sorrow, and pleasure, and refine your thinking.

雲が湧き風は流れる　そして光も宿る
かすみたつ山なみを庭にして　今日がはじまる
Clouds Arise, Wind flows and Light Dwells
The day starts anew as I look over a misty mountain range, behind the garden

はるかな山なみと対峙するスミエスクは、今日と真摯に向き合い
明日に向かって歩を進めることを願っている。
「たとえ明日世界が滅びるとしても私はリンゴの木を植えるだろう」と述べた
マルティン・ルターの言葉のように ―――
それがスミエスクの私たちへのメッセージ。

マルティン・ルター　1483年―1546年　ドイツの宗教家

Viewing the mountain range in the distance, Sumiesque hopes that we will live each day to its fullest and strive forward for a better tomorrow.
As Martin Luther said, "Even if I knew that tomorrow the world would go to pieces, I would still plant my apple tree."
That is a message from Sumiesque to us.

Martin Luther (1483 - 1546) German theologian

あ と が き

Epilogue

あ と が き

　"もぢずりの花" が古今集のなかで詠まれていることを知ったのは
この春のこと。

　私の幼い頃、この花は "ねじり花" と呼ばれていました。
春になると野原や草むらに螺旋状のピンクの小花をつけかわいい姿で
咲いていたものです。
　それから数十年以上ねじり花を見かけることはなかったので、
この世から消えてしまったものとばかり思っていました。
ところが、数年前に引っ越したわが家の庭先でたまたま "ねじり花" を見つけ、
驚きと懐かしさに心が躍りました。

　本書の制作に多大なご尽力をいただいたヨシタミチコ氏から
「万葉人はこの花を "もぢずりの花" と呼び、古くから親しんでいた」
ということを聞きました。
広大な宇宙に包まれ、長い時の流れのなかで生きつづける自然界の神秘。
その生命の営みに心打たれる思いがいたしました。
　ヨシタミチコ氏は、色彩の世界を言葉に、それも美しい詩文にかえて
スミエスクを格調高く謳いあげて下さいました。
素敵な出会いに恵まれたことに心より感謝申し上げます。

A f t e r w o r d

I happened to discover that "Mojizuri no hana" (Autumn lady s-tresses) are depicted in a poem in the *Kokinshu* (Japanese anthology of poetry).

When I was a young child, this flower was called "Nejiri bana".
In the spring, these cute flowers with a rosette of pink florets used to bloom in fields and grass.

Since then, decades have passed, and I haven't seen any Nejiri bana flowers, so I thought they had disappeared from the earth. However, I happened to find some Nejiri bana flowers in the garden of my new house that I moved into a few years ago. I was surprised, and my heart was filled with delight upon finding the flower again.

I heard from Ms. Michiko Yoshita, who helped me a great deal in producing this book, that the Manyo people called this flower the "Mojizuri no hana", and have cherished it for generations.

They are surrounded by a vast expanse, and they have survived for a tremendous amount of time. I felt the wonder of nature, and I was struck by the sustainability of these flowers.

Ms. Michiko Yoshita transformed the feeling of their colors into words, which became like beautiful and elegant poetry, with the subject of Sumiesque. I am thankful that I was fortunate enough to be able to meet Ms. Michiko Yoshita, who is exceptionally sensible and deeply thoughtful.

ある時、不思議と味わいのある水墨画に心が惹かれました。

長谷川等伯の「松林図屏風」画です。

七尾の海から見た松林は、薄ずみ色の濃淡とぼかしによる

松のシルエットが霧の中に点在してうかぶ情景。

それはまさに幻と現（うつつ）の境域に見え隠れする

幽玄の世界そのものでした。

　「松林図屏風」画と出会い、水墨のはかり知れない奥深さを知ったとき、

私は、墨の独特な色合いをもつ花をつくりたいと思いました。

中国の水墨画の長い歴史と文化を熟知された香港の生産業者は、

仕上げ加工の技術を駆使し私が思い描いた墨の色を忠実に表現して下さいました。

そして誕生した花のグループが「Sumiesque（スミエスク）」です。

私は墨の趣を追求したスミエスクが造花の究極の花であると確信しています。

　時を越え悠久の墨色を見つめ、

花たちと語り合ったフラワーデザイナーの皆さま方のご尽力に感謝するとともに、

新しい造花の空間装飾を担われる方々の益々のご活躍を祈念申し上げます。

これを機に、装飾造花の明日が大きく拡がる世界であることを信じています。

　最後になりましたが、本書の制作にあたり、多くの助言をいただき

長時間の作業にも労を惜しまず向きあってくださった編集スタッフの皆さまに

深く感謝の意を表したいと思います。

皆さまありがとうございました。

山田　波子

At that time, I was attracted to an ink painting that had a mysterious look to it.

The picture was called "Pine Forest View Folding Screen", and was made by Tohaku Hasegawa.

The picture shows a silhouette of pine trees in the fog that are emerging into view from the sea of Nanac, and it is painted in thick, thin, and blurry black ink. It shows a subtle and profound world that seems to exist between illusion and reality.

Inspired by the world of this Chinese ink painting, I started to think that I wanted to create flowers in unique shades of colors.

A Hong Kong producer who is knowledgeable about longstanding Chinese ink paintings and the sophisticated culture related to them, helped me to produce the flowers exactly as I envisaged them, making full use of producer's technology. Thus, a group of flowers named "Sumiesque" was born.

I firmly believe that Sumiesque is the ultimate flower amongst all the artificial flowers.

I would like to thank the floral designers, who worked hard, while looking at the eternity of the world beyond time to interact with the flowers. I also hope that these people will be more and more active in the new field of space decoration with artificial flowers.

I wish that this occasion would bring an expanding world for decorative artificial flowers in the future.

Last but not least, I would also like to thank the editorial staff members who provided much of their time and gave me valuable advice in producing this book.

I sincerely appreciate everyone's support.

Namiko Yamada

協 力 者 一 覧　　［五十音順］

伊藤 美奈子［いとう みなこ］

株式会社アスカ商会の企画部に13年間勤務。2004年に独立し、アーティフィシャルフラワープランニング"soup"（スープ）を設立。ダイナミックでモダンなデザインを得意とする。インテリアとなるオブジェスタイルを目指しており、現在もディスプレーからデザインアレンジなど幅広く手がけている。

伊庭 麻理子［いば まりこ］

東京都出身、主婦。アーティフィシャルフラワーの自由で豊かな世界に魅了され、愛着ある表現をテーマに創作している。オンラインショップでの販売、オーダー中心の制作活動。

柏山 加世子［かしやま かよこ］

北海道旭川市生まれ。華道未生会、中央フラワーにて花の道に入る。1968年、華道未生会師範、中央フラワーアーティスト1級取得。1971年、教室と並行し、アーティフィシャルフラワーの専門店「フラワーショップかしやま」を開店。1983年、トータルフラワー協会設立に携わり、1987年まで年1回のペースで展示会を開催。1989年、トータルフラワー協会2代目会長就任。2002年より2014年まで旭川グランドホテルのフラワーコンサルタントを勤める。アーティフィシャルフラワーアレンジメントの制作販売のほか、生花アレンジメント、店舗ディスプレー、会場装花、華道及びフラワーアレンジメントの教室を開くなど精力的に活動している。

装花草庵［そうか そうあん］

1997年より、東京・吉祥寺を中心に、アーティフィシャルフラワーによる空間デザインを手がける。美しさと寂しさ、強さと繊細さ、光と影、永遠と瞬間、世界にひそむ両極の姿を表現することを目指し、装花だけでなく空間全体を印象付ける背景や小物なども製作。Flower Art Showcase Award 2014 in Tokyo Midtown優秀作品賞、東京ミッドタウン賞受賞。

山本 純子［やまもと じゅんこ］

多摩美術大学彫刻科卒業。1996年より2007年まで中部行動美術展に出展し、佳作賞・奨励賞など受賞。同時期、中部総合美術展・個展においても彫刻作品を出展。2002年より現在まで毎年画廊企画展において彫金作品を出展。元名古屋造形大学短期大学部非常勤講師。現在は、株式会社アスカ商会にデザイナーとして勤務。

山本 のり子［やまもと のりこ］

1964年ジュリアン株式会社を父・山本永昇が設立。東京・吉祥寺でジュリアンカルチャースクールを経営。母・山本薫よりアーティフィシャルフラワーを学ぶ。2003年、三好雅子氏（IAD国際アートフラワーデザイナー協会理事）と出会い、フランスのアーティフィシャルフラワーの美しさに魅せられる。2009年、パリでの研修を経てディプロマを取得。2012年から、年に一度のペースでアーティフィシャルフラワーアレンジ教室の展示即売会を開催している。

墨画　山田 由美子［やまだ ゆみこ］

1961年国立音楽大学卒業後、2014年までピアノ教授に。1965年、女流画家協会展に初出品し入選。以後、7年連続入選。1969年には福島県展に入選。1994年旅のスケッチ展を主宰。2005年、朝日新聞社主催銀座展に入賞。2009年、水墨画を松下黄沙氏に学び、墨画グループ82に所属。2011年には、東京交通会館ギャラリーにて個展を開催。2012年、横浜赤レンガ倉庫にて14人展に出展。2012年の灯芸術展において、初出品し入賞を飾ると、2015年まで連続入賞。審査員も兼ねる。現在は旅のスケッチクラブ代表。墨画グループ82、東京灯芸術協会の所属。